For my wife, with love.

***Andrew Wild** lists his interests as: local history, walking, architecture, art, literature, music and travel. He is a stage manager for Macclesfield Amateur Dramatics Society and has also worked in productions for the Paragon Youth Theatre and Heald Green Theatre. He is a member of Macclesfield Civic Society, is married, and works as a personal computer network analyst for a large Wilmslow-based insurance company.*

***Thanks to:** Amanda Wild and David Ratcliffe (for test walking, often under duress), Malcolm Bell and Steve Johnson (for advice and support), Clive Cranshaw (for proof reading and equipment loan), Rod Hackney and Nicholas Winterton (for their time and enthusiasm), Doug Pickford (for the pictures of "Old Macclesfield") and Graham Beech and all at Sigma Press.*

108 Steps Around Macclesfield

Andrew Wild

Published by Sigma Leisure - an imprint of
Sigma Press, 1 South Oak Lane, Wilmslow, Cheshire SK9 6AR, England.

British Library Cataloguing in Publication Data
A CIP record for this book is available from the British Library.

ISBN: 1-85058-436-2

Typesetting and Design by: Sigma Press, Wilmslow, Cheshire.

Printed by: Manchester Free Press

Cover design: The Agency, Wilmslow

Cover photograph: The 108 Steps, Macclesfield (Chris Rushton)

Photographs and line drawings: Andrew Wild

Foreword

I read Andrew Wild's book, *108 Steps Around Macclesfield*, with absolute fascination. His detailed research and accurate descriptions bring vividly to life many of the commercial and residential buildings, open spaces, schools, churches, streets and other features of the Town.

His book is an invaluable asset to all of us who wish to know more about Macclesfield and its history, as well as to those many thousands of visitors who come every year.

How many of us will have the stamina to complete the walk in one go remains to be seen, but the joy of Andrew Wild's approach is that the walk can be done a little at a time in order to fully appreciate the depth of the research which he has undertaken.

This is an essential reference work for local scholars, residents and walkers alike, and I gladly commend it to all.

Nicholas R Winterton

Member of Parliament for Macclesfield

Contents

Introduction

Macclesfield is out to fox the visitor. Passing train travellers would never dream of the delights it offers if only they were fortunate to have to stop and take a look. Macclesfield's ugliest building, the railway station, offers no clues, but simply reinforces sceptical prejudices. The Victoria Park flats, designed in Denmark (I thought they were good at design in Scandinavia) confirms these prejudices. But walk away, uphill into the town centre or the other way towards the Canal and a charming yet vibrant world of fine buildings and good natured people will be revealed.

Macclesfield is a tantalising paradox. Strangers and even the locals would perhaps struggle to be told that they are in a town with Britain's lowest unemployment rate and which boasts a top ten position in the wealthy league. *The Times* newspaper blurts; "Some northern towns do penetrate the south dominated ... prosperity table and these include Macclesfield." *The Guardian*, not to be outdone, offers us a reason; "A power-house for the self-employed." and *The Telegraph*; "Macclesfield has become prosperous by developing ... local economies."

This walking guide leads you to understand why the town is so vibrant, vital and well-off. Many of the buildings in Macclesfield have been saved from almost certain demolition by forward-thinking Macclesfield people and an enlightened Macclesfield Borough Council. For example, Paradise Street, the Heritage Centre, Charles Roe House, the Macclesfield Arms, the Black Road Schemes, 19 King Edward Street and the Manchester, Liverpool and District Bank which has been converted into the town's new library. As you will see, all these buildings have been included in the walk.

Several other buildings which have not been under threat but are important to the town would include the Savage and Legh

Chapels of St Michael's, Arighi Bianchi, Macclesfield United Reform Church, Christ Church, Fairstead House on Bridge Street, St Alban's, The King's School, Cumberland House, Jordangate House and King Edward Street Unitarian Chapel. These, too, and many others, are included in the walk.

Good Walking!

Rod Hackney

Macclesfield, 1994

A Short History of Macclesfield

Stone, Bronze and Iron-Age settlements have been identified around Macclesfield, Roman roads run through the area and Britons named local features such as Kerridge and the Dane, but The Domesday Survey of 1086 provides the first written reference to the town. The first settlement in Macclesfield, where the Market Place is now situated was, by tradition, first called Hameston, or "the settlement on the rock". It is not known how, why or when the village became known as Macclesfield, but Macca is a Saxon personal name and may have given rise to "Macca's Field". Macclesfield was certainly the name of the town in the Domesday Book. The town, once a prosperous and wealthy farming settlement, and part of the lands of Edwin, Earl of Mercia, was decimated by William the Conqueror and his army during the suppression of the Northern English in 1068. William gave the Earldom of Chester, which included the village of Macclesfield, to his nephew Hugh.

The town recovered and grew to become the most important in East Cheshire and was established as a Borough in 1220. The seventh Earl of Chester, John, died in 1238 without male heirs and the earldom was taken by Henry III as "We are unwilling so illustrious an inheritance should fall under the divided sway of the distaffs of women." The Earldom, and therefore the town of Macclesfield, thus became crown property. The first royal patron was Henry's eldest son, Prince Edward, later Edward I, who granted a charter to the town at Guildford in May 1261. Edward gave the manor of Macclesfield to his wife, Eleanor of Castile, as part of her dowry and she consecrated the first chapel, later St Michael's and All Angels, in 1278.

John de Macclesfield, a minister of Richard II, built a castellated mansion house in the town at the end of the fourteenth century. The uncertainties of the Wars of the Roses gave rise to two influential families in the fifteenth and sixteenth centuries - The Leghs of Lyme Hall and the Savages of the Lord's Park, Gawsworth. They each built chapels for their family tombs in the parish church. The Battle of Flodden field in 1513, when the English were victorious against the Scots, cost Macclesfield its Mayor, Christopher Savage, and all his leading men.

There was a considerable amount of building and rebuilding in the town during the sixteenth century and new charters were granted by Elizabeth I in 1564 and 1595. Macclesfield began to expand its medieval borders in the seventeenth century with new industries being introduced, such as harness-making, leather glove-making and the manufacture of silk buttons. The fairs and market attracted buyers and sellers from a very wide area and the village expanded and developed into a country town.

Civil War broke out in England in 1642 and continued until the defeat of the King by Parliament in 1648. Towns with growing industries were generally against the King, but Macclesfield was on the periphery of both sides' holdings and was of some strategic importance. It was occupied by the Royalists in 1642 and taken by the Parliamentary Army in February 1643. The monarchy was restored under Charles II in 1660 who granted a charter to the town in 1684.

Prince Charles Edward Stuart, or Bonnie Prince Charlie, the pretender to the Hanover throne, twice visited Macclesfield in December 1745. He was marching from Scotland to London to lay claim to the throne on behalf of his father, James. Their hereditary claims were stronger than that of George II, but the constitution of England did not allow Roman Catholics to occupy the throne. An army of between six and seven thousand men occupied the town on 3rd December commandeering as many men, arms and ammunition and as much corn, hay and provisions as they could. The army reached Derby before turning back. Word reached the people of Macclesfield the day before the army was due and many people, including the mayor and many officials, left the town in fright. The remaining inhabitants were plundered and robbed by the army when it returned. The Scots stayed for three days before making their way back to Scotland and eventual defeat at Culloden. The Duke of Cumberland, the second son of George II, stayed in Macclesfield on 10th December 1745 during his pursuit of the Scots.

Charles Roe was the most significant influence on the development of the town during the second half of the eighteenth century. Roe had come to Macclesfield from Castleton in Derbyshire by 1742 and, in 1743-4, built the town's first silk mill, powered by water, on the corner of Mill Street and Park Green. His copper works was established in 1758. He funded the construction of Christ Church in 1774-5 and died in 1781 leaving a large fortune.

The fortunes of the silk industry fluctuated however. England was at war with France intermittently throughout the eighteenth century. French competition during the years of peace resulted in the depression of the English silk industry. Many firms were hit particularly hard in the period following the Seven Years' War that ended in 1763. Charles Roe had recovered all of his silk-based capital in 1760 and, by 1773, the company he founded was bankrupt.

Silk weaving and steam driven machinery were introduced to the town in the last decade of the eighteenth century. Many of the mills and three-storey weavers garrets which can be seen throughout the town date from the end of the eighteenth and beginning of the nineteenth centuries. The period of the Napoleonic Wars between 1793 and 1815 was a time of great expansion for the town. This was followed by a period of acute depression and a boom in the early 1820s. Over seventy mills had been built in the town for silk or cotton manufacture by this time. Macclesfield became preeminent in silk manufacture after about 1850 when other local towns, such as Manchester and Stockport, ceased to produce silk. Macclesfield had very little industry other than silk and had little choice but to continue its production. Its excellence in producing silk goods resulted in the epithet "Silk Town".

The Parliamentary Reform Act of 1832 had a particular significance for Macclesfield with the election of its first MP, John Brocklehurst, who represented a population of over 30,000. The previous year had seen the opening of the Macclesfield Canal, one of the last of the inland waterways which connected the town with the Trent & Mersey canal at Kidsgrove and the Peak Forest canal at Marple. The town's first railway was opened from Manchester in 1845, with links to the Potteries four years later.

The Victorian expansion of the town (13,000 inhabitants in 1811; 37,500 in 1881) led to the construction of many new churches and chapels in and around the centre of the town: St George's (1822), Bethel Baptist Chapel (1822), Brunswick Chapel (1823), Kidd's Chapel (1829), Park Street Chapel (1836), Newtown Methodist Chapel (1837), Holy Trinity, Hurdsfield (1839), St Alban's (1839), St Paul's (1843), St Peter's (1849), Frost's Chapel (1858), St George's Street Baptist Chapel (1873), United Reform Church (1877) and the Spiritualist Chapel (1879). The increase in inhabitants also led to the increase in the number of public houses in the town, with over two hundred being licensed in 1840.

During the Second World War Macclesfield's silk industry made a huge contribution to the war effort when many mills were used for the production of parachutes, uniforms and mosquito nets.

The silk industry still survives in Macclesfield, but many mills have been demolished and those that survive are mostly used for other industry. The nearby sites of Zeneca and Ciba-Geigy provide much employment for the town. There has been a large increase in self-employment in recent years and over 1 in 10 of Macclesfield's inhabitants have their own businesses.

Macclesfield of the 1990s has, like many other towns, inherited a number of indifferent or poorly designed buildings from the 1960s and 1970s (one immediately thinks of Stuart House on King Edward Street, Marks & Spencer on Mill Street, Victoria Park Flats, London & Manchester House on Park Street and the Magnet showrooms on Churchill Way) but the rearrangement of the county, district and borough councils in 1974 has resulted in conscientious and sympathetic town planning. Most of the buildings constructed since 1974 have been built in materials appropriate to the town and in a manner which is appropriate to the existing buildings of the town.

A committed effort has been made to conserve the older buildings of the town with buildings such as Charles Roe House (built in the 18th century), the Heritage Centre (1813-4), the District Bank (1881) and Paradise Street (early 19th century) being not only saved from almost certain demolition but also being renovated and put to appropriate uses. This process is continuing with the current or proposed renovations to Christ Church (1775), 19 King Edward Street (1798) and the Macclesfield Arms (18th century).

A number of conservation areas have been designated around the town centre to safeguard the future of Macclesfield's legacy of Georgian and Victorian buildings. The conservation areas were set up to preserve and enhance the special character of the town and have strict rules governing proposed external alterations of the buildings in them.

Macclesfield can, in the 1990s, be proud of its history and its policy of creating and maintaining a worthwhile environment for the future generations of Maxonians.

Serious scholars of Macclesfield's history should refer to "A History of Macclesfield" edited by C. Stella Davies, published by the University Of Manchester Press in 1961, reprinted by E.J. Morten (Publishers) in 1981, and "Streets and Houses of Old Macclesfield" by John Earles, first published in 1915 and reprinted by MTD Rigg Publications in 1990. Both volumes are available for lending in the public library.

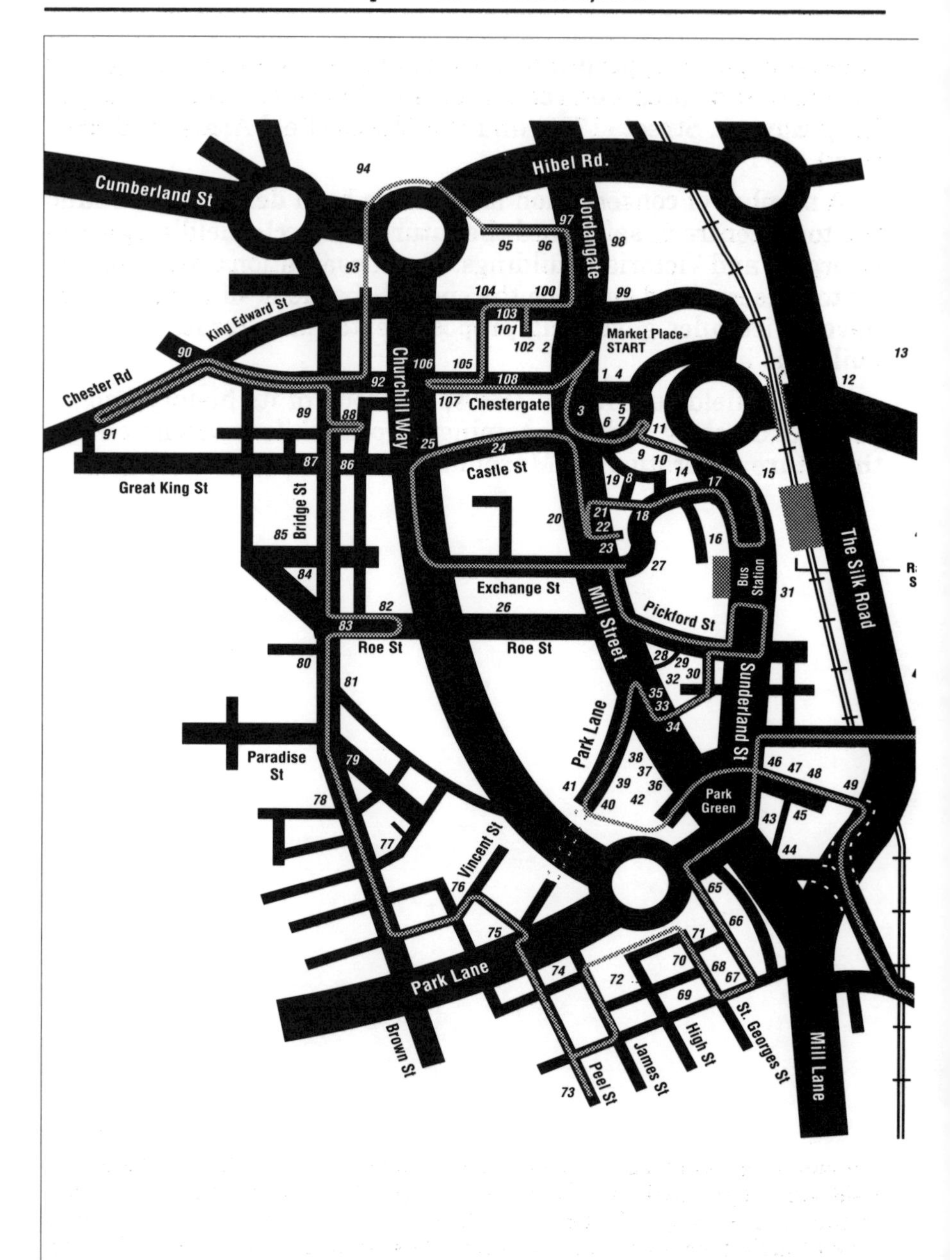
Cumberland St
Hibel Rd.
Jordangate
King Edward St
Chester Rd
Churchill Way
Market Place-
START
Chestergate
Castle St
Great King St
Bridge St
Exchange St
Mill Street
Bus Station
Pickford St
Roe St
Roe St
Sunderland St
The Silk Road
Park Lane
Paradise St
Park Green
Vincent St
Park Lane
Brown St
Peel St
James St
High St
St. Georges St
Mill Lane

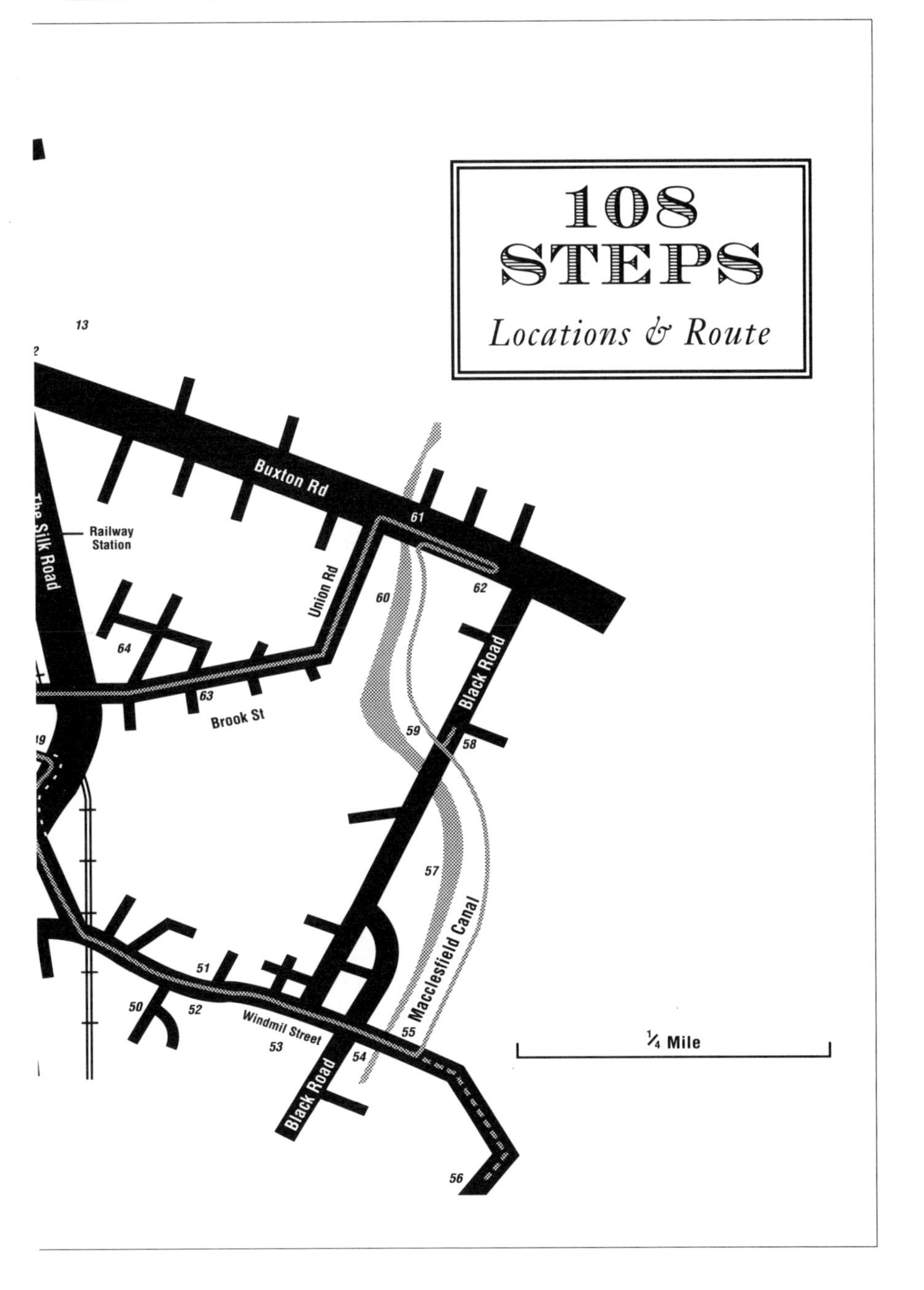

108
STEPS
Locations & Route
13
Buxton Rd
The Silk Road
Railway Station
Union Rd
61
60
62
64
Black Road
63
Brook St
59
58
57
Macclesfield Canal
51
50
52
Windmil Street
53
55
54
Black Road
56
¼ Mile

108 STEPS: The Main Walk

Approximate duration: three and a half hours

The 108 Steps Around Macclesfield Town Walk begins and ends at the Town Hall Information Centre, but as it is circular it can begin at Roe Street Heritage Centre (26), Park Green (44), the Railway Station (15), the Bus Station (opposite 31), St Michael's (5), Christ Church (85) or any one of the 108 locations featured. A number of shorter walks have been included for those pushed for time or short of breath. These walks are towards the back of this book.

1. **THE TOWN HALL** has been built in three stages. The first part, which faces St Michael's church, was built in 1823-4 and designed by Francis Goodwin. The Hall was extended in 1869-71 with a new façade (designed by James Stevens) opposite the end of Chestergate, and again in 1991-2 towards Jordangate. The new extension was opened by the Duke of York in December 1992. A Tudor Guildhall that previously occupied the site was demolished to make way for the new Town Hall in 1823. The red telephone boxes outside the building are "listed as buildings of architectural or historical significance".

The Town Hall (1) and Market Place (3)

Facing the Town Hall extension is

2. **THE BULL'S HEAD,** an eighteenth century coaching inn that served coaches on the Manchester, Birmingham and London route.

Return past the Town Hall to:

3. **THE OLD MARKET PLACE.** This irregular square is the heart of medieval Macclesfield. The various ages of the buildings around it are testimony to its constant evolution. The market cross was removed from the Market Place in 1795 when it was bought by a local farmer who used part of it as shaft for a land-roller and the rest as a gravestone for one of his dogs. The inscription "MWW 1798" dates from this time. It was moved to West Park in 1858 and returned to the Market Place earlier this century.

The Borough Police Station (4)

Walk through the church gates and into the yard. Next to the town hall to the left of the church can be seen the

4. **BOROUGH POLICE STATION**, built in 1900 to replace a previous building on the site dating from 1874. The Macclesfield Borough Police Force merged with the Cheshire Constabulary in 1947. The police station is now on Brunswick Street, on the far side of the Town Hall from here.

5. **ST. MICHAEL'S AND ALL ANGELS.** This, Macclesfield's parish church, has a long and complex history. It was founded by Eleanor of Castile, wife of Edward I, as St Allowes or All Hallows in 1278, a daughter church to St Peter's in Prestbury. Edward and Eleanor made frequent visits to the town having both a manor house and hunting lodge nearby. The original church had a simple four-bay battlemented nave, a two-bay chancel, a tower with a spire added later and a south porch. Some of the original stones of the south porch were retained during the most recent reconstruction and the mark of the consecrating Bishop of St Asaph's (who was acting for the Bishop of Lichfield and Coventry in whose diocese Macclesfield then was) can still be seen. It is a small circle with a cross within. The Legh Chapel (7) was added in 1422 to the south side of the church, followed in 1502-7 by the Savage Chapel (6). The original church remained substantially the same until 1739 when the nave and chancel were replaced by an extravagant new church in the popular classical style of the time. A peal of bells was installed in the tower at this time and the church was re-dedicated to St Michael. The classical style was not popular with the Victorians who decided to rebuild the main part of the church again. A revival of the Perpendicular style (mid 14th - mid 16th centuries) was chosen and designed by Sir Arthur Blomfield. The foundation stone was laid by the Duke of Westminster in 1898 and the church was completed in 1901. Stone from the classical church was reused to face the tower (the spire had been removed around the time of the first rebuilding). The medieval Legh and Savage Chapels

St Michael's before the 1898-1901 rebuilding (photo courtesy of Doug Pickford)

St Michael's (5) as it is today

have survived two complete rebuildings of the main part of the church and are Macclesfield's oldest church buildings. To the left of the west door, inside the church, can be seen the responds of the original nave (where the arch springs from its supporting column), all that remains of Queen Eleanor's church.

Go to the right of the church tower.

6. **THE SAVAGE CHAPEL**, with its distinctive three-storey porch, was built between 1502 and 1507. It was built and endowed as a chantry chapel by Thomas Savage, Archbishop of York, who was a local man and married Henry VII's eldest son, Prince Arthur, to Catherine of Aragon at York Minster. The chancel of the main part of the church and the Savage Chapel itself contain seven recumbent effigies of the members of the Savage family, dating from the late fifteenth to the late seventeenth centuries. The famous Pardon Brass can also be seen here. It was erected to the memory of Roger Legh and his wife in 1506 and is the only known instance of the Mass of St Gregory on a monumental brass. The chapel also has a splendid canted east window. Thomas Savage was buried in York Minster but his heart was brought to Macclesfield and interred in the walls of the Savage Chapel.

7. **THE LEGH CHAPEL** is not very evident from the outside. Look for the series of nine windows to the left of the Savage Chapel porch. It was built in 1422 to receive the body of Piers Legh of Lyme Hall who fought at Agincourt in 1415 and was knighted on the field. He died in Paris from wounds received in the siege of Meaux. A brass on the wall of the chapel commemorates Piers Legh and his father.

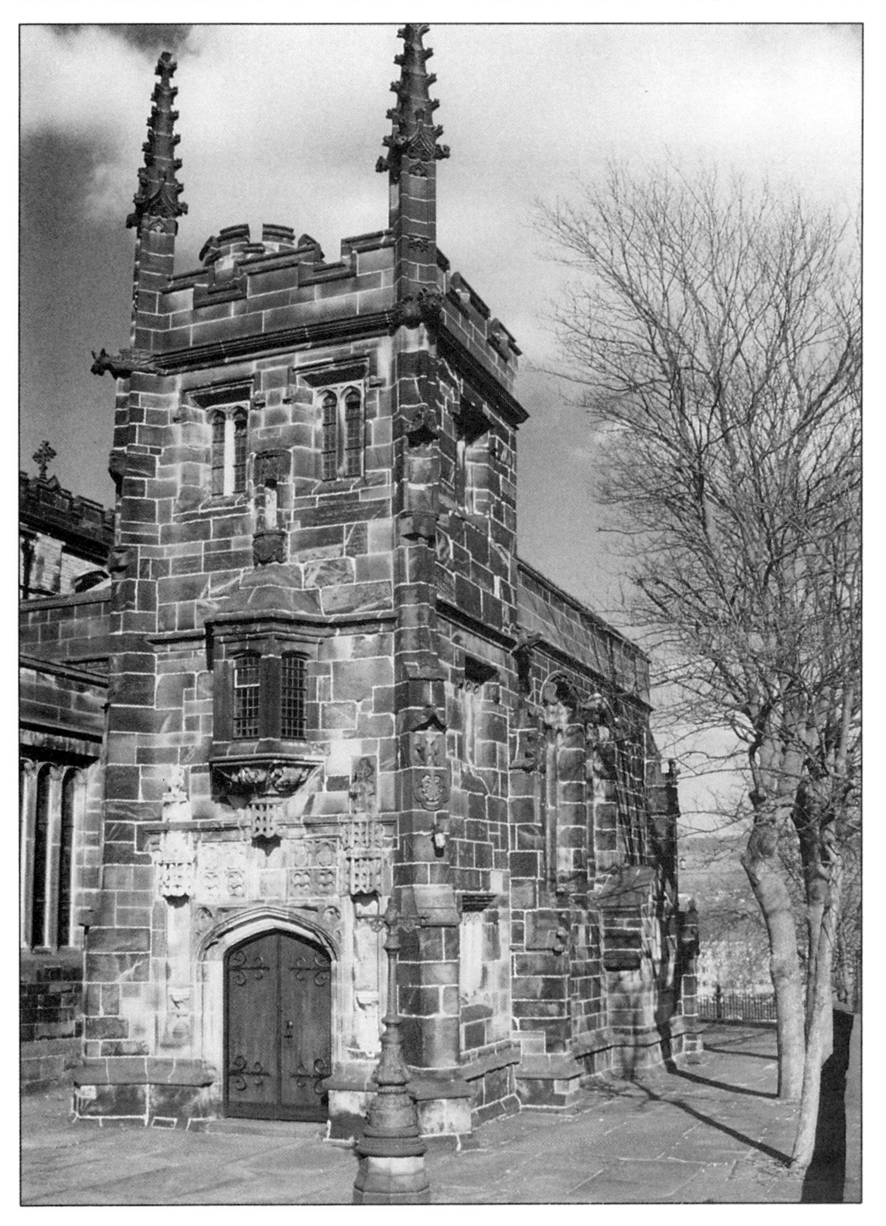

The Savage Chapel (6)

Return to the Market Place and start walking down the steep and cobbled Church Street (to the left as you leave the church gates).

8. **CHURCH STREET.** Once called Churchwallgate, a town gate was sited at the top of the street on the corner of the Market Place. This narrow street has been widened twice, the first time in 1818 when the gate was removed, and again in 1939. The dates are commemorated on stone plaques on the wall next to Bridgford's.

Turn left along Churchside.

9. **No 43 CHURCHSIDE** is believed to have been the town house of the Leghs of Lyme Hall. The house is eighteenth century with a Regency (early 19th century) façade. Churchside has long been favoured by the legal profession. The street was originally known as Le Dede Street, literally the street of the dead, and later Churchyard Street.

Continue along Churchside to the top of the steps. On the right here, is:

10. **ST. MICHAEL TERRACE.** A row of houses squeezed onto a small plot. The house at the far end dates from the sixteenth century.

Walk round to the left to the small park and the site of the

11. **OLD GRAMMAR SCHOOL.** This small park (officially called the Brocklehurst Memorial Gardens but commonly known as Sparrow Park) was once the site of the Old Grammar School that was founded in 1502. The Macclesfield Grammar school was one of the earliest school foundations, receiving an endowment and a charter dated 1552 constituting it "The Free Grammar School of King Edward the Sixth in Macclesfield". It was re-sited to King Edward Street in 1748 and to its current site on Cumberland Street in 1856 (94). The last of the

original buildings was demolished as recently as the beginning of this century. The site was given to the town in 1905.

Walk to the low wall on the opposite side of the park to the gate. From here can be seen:

12. **ARIGHI, BIANCHI.** The furniture company was formed in 1854 and this, their showroom, dates from the late nineteenth century and has a fine cast iron and glass façade. The building is on the site of the town workhouse which was later moved and developed into West Park Hospital.

And behind,

13. **VICTORIA PARK FLATS**, the town centre's only deck-access or high rise housing, dating from the late 1960s.

Return to the top of the steps:

14. **108 STEPS.** These are the famous 108 steps of Macclesfield, also once known as School Brow or Bank due to the location of the Grammar School at their head.

Count them! At the end of the alley that leads from the foot of the steps, turn right and cross the road to:

15. **THE RAILWAY STATION.** The first railway to reach Macclesfield was the London & North Western Railway that opened a temporary station on Beech Road for services from Manchester in 1845. This station was replaced by Hibel Road station in 1849 a month after services commenced south on the lines to Congleton and Leek that were operated by the North Staffordshire Railway. Macclesfield Station (still shown as Central on some maps despite being renamed upon the closure of Hibel Road in 1960) was opened by the Macclesfield,

The 108 Steps (14)

Bollington & Marple Railway in 1873. A temporary station had been in use next to the site since passenger traffic commenced two years before. The line to Bollington and Marple closed in 1970. The southern half has been used for the A523 (Silk Road) and the northern half is now the Middlewood Way footpath.

Opposite is:

16. **THE QUEEN'S HOTEL.** A newly restored staging inn built in 1875 and named in honour of Queen Victoria whose image is above the door. This end of Waters Green was renamed Albert Place after the Queen's consort, a nameplate can be seen on the last building before the bus station on this side of the road. John Wesley preached near here in 1747 leading to the establishment of Methodism in the town.

Return to the open area of

17. **WATERS GREEN.** The site of the town well, cattle market and annual fairs is so called due to the once-frequent flooding of the nearby River Bollin (49). The fairs were the Barnaby Fair (held on St Barnabas' Day, June 11th) and All Soul's Day Fair (November 2nd). Waters Green is still the site of one of Macclesfield's two outdoor markets. The old name "Waters" can be seen on the side of the Old Millstone Inn.

Turn left into Waters Green, following the main road, then right along narrow, steep Backwallgate (look for street name):

18. **BACKWALLGATE.** This street led, in medieval times, from the town's main street to the town well. "Wall" is a corruption of "Well" and "Gate" was the medieval word for "Street".

Half way up Backwallgate, on the right, is

19. THE CASTLE PUBLIC HOUSE. Named after Macclesfield's castle (23), the castle key can still be seen above the bar.

Continue to the top of Backwallgate.

20. MILL STREET. Macclesfield's main shopping street. The buildings here are mostly nineteenth century with twentieth century lower storey façades. Look above the shop fronts for an indication of the age of the buildings.

Turning left into Mill Street from Backwallgate, the first building is:

21. MOTHERCARE. A splendid Georgian brick building that has been somewhat spoiled by the addition of the shop-front. Marks & Spencer's used this shop for many years before moving across the road. Look above the shop-front to the pediment with castle motif.

And next door:

22. ROSE'S. A timber-framed building with a nineteenth century façade.

Turn left along the alley next to Rose's.

23. MACCLESFIELD CASTLE. This area is the site of the yard of Macclesfield Castle. It was actually a castellated mansion built in the last decade of the fourteenth century by John de Macclesfield, an official at the court of Richard II and a minister of the royal household. It covered an area of approximately one quarter of an acre on the site of Marks and Spencer's with a garden and orchard of one acre surrounded by a stone wall by the side of Backwallgate. The mansion passed from John de Macclesfield to his son, John, and then to the Staffords,

Dukes Of Buckingham. It was altered and enlarged during the latter part of the sixteenth century and at about that time it passed into the property of the Stanleys, Earls of Derby. The mansion fell into disrepair in the seventeenth century and the few stones that remain can be seen in the courtyard of the Town Hall.

Mothercare, Mill Street (21)

Return along Mill Street (passing Backwallgate on your right) and turn first left into:

24. CASTLE STREET. This street was built as recently as 1923, the foundation stone can be seen on the right-hand side of the street.

Continue to the end of Castle Street to, on the right-hand corner:

25. CHESHIRE BUILDING SOCIETY. This French-influenced building was constructed in 1925-6 as the town's Post Office. It was successfully renovated in 1978-9. Their modern offices opposite were built in 1983-4.

Cheshire Building Society (25)

Turn left from Castle Street along Churchill Way, and stop at the next road left, Exchange Street. The building in front of you is:

26. ROE STREET HERITAGE CENTRE (formerly Sunday School). The Macclesfield Sunday School was instituted in 1796 on Pickford Street but was so successful that by 1812 it operated on five premises. This imposing building was built in 1813-4 from donations given by locals, teachers and students. It was saved from demolition in the late seventies and restored and is now a museum and concert hall.

The Heritage Centre (26)

Turn into Exchange Street and go straight across Mill Street into Queen Victoria Street.

27. **EL RIO DANCE HALL.** A fine view across the Bollin Valley to St Paul's and hills at the edge of the Peak District is afforded here. The car park as Queen Victoria Street bears left is the site of the El Rio Dance Hall (more commonly known as The Liberal Club), the venue of the Beatles' only concert in Macclesfield on 26th January 1963. Their second single "Please Please Me" had been released two weeks before.

A view from Queen Victoria Street (27) showing St Paul's (64), Hovis Mill (60) and Wesley's Chapel (31)

Return to Mill Street, continuing left. Stop opposite the next road right (Roe Street). Along the alley opposite the end of Roe Street (between the two buildings on Mill Street) is the

28. FRIENDS MEETING HOUSE, built in 1703, now used as a snooker club. The Friends now meet at a house in Great King Street.

Go down Pickford Street (opposite Roe Street). Continue to Wood Street (on the right).

29. WOOD STREET MILL, built in 1932, is one of the few remaining mills in this once crowded part of the town. Wood Street was named after the two brothers (Charles and Samuel Wood) who originally owned the first mill on this site, and others in the town, and who were both mayors of the town in the early nineteenth century.

Next to the mill, along Pickford Street, is:

30. THE DAMS BROOK. Still culverted, this brook powered Charles Roe's first silk mill (35).

Continue along Pickford Street and turn second left into Sunderland Street. Along here, on the right, see

31. WESLEY'S CHAPEL (now a Snooker Club). Built in 1779, rebuilt in 1799 and enlarged in 1808, this large brick Georgian building was the first Methodist chapel to be built in Macclesfield. It was built to replace a meeting house on Commercial Road that had been used since 1764. Sunderland Street was known as The Heyes when the chapel was built, due to its rural surroundings.

Return along Sunderland Street, and back into Pickford Street. Turn first left into Charlotte Street and right into Townley Street. On the right here, is:

32. EBENEZER CHAPEL. One of the oldest surviving church buildings in Macclesfield, the Ebenezer (or Townley Street) Chapel was built in 1787-8. The building was extended along Townley Street when a Sunday School extension was added in 1802. Services were transferred to the new Park Green Chapel (now Macclesfield United Reform Church (33)) in 1877 and the Ebenezer Chapel became its church hall, a function it retains.

Take the alley through the gates opposite the Chapel by the side of the church. If these gates are locked, return along Townley Street, and take the alley almost immediately on the right. Turn right at the end of the alley to the front of the church.

33. MACCLESFIELD UNITED REFORM CHURCH. A fine example of Victorian Gothic architecture built in 1877 by C.O. Ellison. The design of the church is a free interpretation of the Medieval Gothic styles of the thirteenth to sixteenth centuries, but breaks all the architectural rules (for what they are) with a symbiotic bravado that is uniquely Victorian. One can only admire the audacity of the architect in flouting six hundred years of building development to create a building so comprehensively 'Victorian'. The interior retains its original fittings and furnishings, including the galleries and an immense pulpit. The site was once occupied by Pickford Hall that, with its extensive grounds, occupied most of this part of town. The UR Church is one of the few worthwhile Victorian buildings in Macclesfield, in complete contrast to,

Next door, you will see

34. BARCLAY'S BANK, built in the Greek Doric Revival style in 1841-2.

On the other side to the church (on the same side of the road), behind the modern office block, is:

35. THE SITE OF MACCLESFIELD'S FIRST SILK MILL, built by Charles Roe in 1744. Silk throwing was introduced to Macclesfield here in 1756. The first steam-powered mill in Macclesfield was built in front of it, along Mill Street, in 1810. This was later known as the Depot Mill when tax refunds were calculated here following the reduction in silk duties in 1824-6. Later, in 1851, a branch of the Manchester, Liverpool & District bank was built here in a bizarre mixture of architectural styles -Baroque, Jacobean and Arts & Crafts. This too has been demolished and a modern branch of the National Westminster Bank occupies the site.

The United Reform Church (33)

ROYAL DEPOT MILLS
ON THIS SITE IN 1744 CHARLES ROE
FOUNDED HIS BUSINESS OF BUTTON
AND TWIST MANUFACTURER
HERE IN 1756 HE INTRODUCED SILK THROWING
INTO THIS TOWN AND PROSPERED
THE SIX STOREY MILL WAS BUILT IN 1810
AND RESTORED IN 1927
THE NEW MILL AT REAR WAS BUILT IN 1932
THIS S.W. WING WAS RECONSTRUCTED IN 1946
BY THE OWNERS J. SWINDELLS LTD.
SILK AND RAYON THROWSTERS
ARTHUR BOSSON PRINCIPAL

The site of the town's first silk mill (35)

Return to the United Reform Church and cross Mill Street. Directly opposite the URC are three buildings, from left to right:

36. THE MACCLESFIELD USEFUL KNOWLEDGE SOCIETY, which is the brick building slightly set back from the others with a bowed upper storey. This eighteenth century building was built as the vicarage of St Michael and was used as such until 1817 when a new one was built on Beech Lane (the continuation of Jordangate). It was later used as a surgery and then purchased in 1850 by the Macclesfield Useful Knowledge Society that had been formed by several managers of Macclesfield Sunday School (Roe Street) in 1833. The Society's art class became the state-aided School of Design in 1852 and, from 1880, part of the building housed the newly formed Girls' High School. The science classes led to the founding of the Technical School (later College) who rented rooms from the Useful Knowledge

Society from 1891. Government funds allowed the School to purchase the premises in 1895 on the understanding that the Girls' High School would not be disturbed for ten years. The Useful Knowledge Society was incorporated into the School the following year, and expansion of the Girls' High School resulted in its relocation to Fence Avenue on the east side of the town in 1909. The building is still part of Macclesfield College.

Next door (actually part of the same building):

37. MACCLESFIELD TECHNICAL SCHOOL. This building is an extension to the older building and was completed in 1899 in a severely contrasting Victorian Gothic style.

The Old Library (38)

Next door is:

38. CHADWICK FREE LIBRARY, built in 1874-6 by local architect James Stevens (who also designed the first extension to the Town Hall and the Infirmary, now demolished) in a style similar to that used for the United Reform Church. It was given to the town by David Chadwick who was MP for Macclesfield at that time. A flight of stone steps led to a double entrance placed on each angle of the projection on the Park Green side of the building. The old 'reading room' has a Gothic window with stained glass and the arms of Chadwick, and the symbol of Macclesfield Corporation below. The library was closed in 1994 upon the opening of a larger replacement library on the corner of Jordangate and the Market Place (99). It has been proposed to use this building as the town's registry office.

Next to the library around the corner on Park Lane is:

39. COLLEGE OF FURTHER EDUCATION, formerly the Macclesfield School of Art where students trained as designers for the silk trade. Dated 1877.

Continue along Park Lane to:

40. PARADISE MILL, a nineteenth century mill built in the 1820s and extended in the 1860s. It housed the last hand-weaving business in the town and closed in 1981. Part of the mill has been converted into a museum and opened to the public in 1984.

Opposite:

41. THE BLUEBERRY INN. This has the name W.A. SMITH & SON on the side. This is the name of one of the six closed breweries of Macclesfield. W.A. Smith of Bond Street were taken over by Marston, Thompson & Evershed in 1962. The other breweries were Harry Evans & Co. of Bond Street who were taken over by

The College of Further Education (39)

Bindley & Co of Burton on Trent in 1890; FW Maurice & Co of the Queen's Brewery, Albert Place, closed c. 1905; C.A. Hordern & Co of the Grapes Brewery, Lord Street, taken over by the North Cheshire Brewery Co. Ltd between 1910 and 1921; the North Cheshire Brewery Co Ltd of Charles Street, founded in 1862 and taken over by Lonsdale and Adshead in 1928; Lonsdale & Adshead Ltd of the Macclesfield Brewery, Park Green, founded in 1790 and taken over by Ind Coope (now Tetley-Carlsberg) in 1950.

Paradise Mill (40)

Take the steps at the side of the overpass, then take the steps down to Parsonage Street. On the left along here (look for the round-arched windows) is:

42. PARSONAGE STREET CHAPEL, built by a splinter group from the Unitarian Chapel on King Edward Street (102) who subsequently rejoined in 1887. The building has since been converted to industrial use. Parsonage

Street is so called because the vicarage of St Michael's stood here (36).

Continue to the end of Parsonage Street, then turn right to the crossroads. Cross to the small park.

43. PARK GREEN WAR MEMORIAL, earlier known as Parsonage Green, developed during the industrial revolution as an open space.

Park Green War Memorial (43), Park Green Mill (44) and Frost's (Park Green) Chapel (45)

Behind the War Memorial is:

44. PARK GREEN MILL, built in 1785, originally ran on water power from the River Bollin (49) which passes behind. The Mill was one of many in Macclesfield that was used for the manufacture of parachutes and other silk goods during the Second World War.

Next door, to the left, see:

45. FROST'S CHAPEL, one of the largest church buildings in the town, was operational between 1858 and 1940 and has been converted to industrial use as part of the adjoining Park Green Mill. It is still known as Chapel Mill but is no longer in use.

The building on the corner of Park Green and Sunderland Street is

46. PARK GREEN HOUSE, a Georgian building with a Dutch gable and Venetian window, it has been a surgery for well over a hundred years.

Park Green House (46) and Georgian House (47)

Next door (on Park Green) is:

47. GEORGIAN HOUSE, built in 1770 as a private mansion and later used as a Library & Reading Room for the better-off and as a Gentlemen's Club.

Next door to this, you find:

48. SILK UNION BUILDING. Macclesfield's first trade union, the Amalgamated Society of Textile Workers and Kindred Trades (formed in 1826) had their headquarters here.

Take the cobbled road on the left-hand side of Frost's Chapel to the footbridge over

49. THE RIVER BOLLIN. The power behind the early silk mills, the Bollin joins the River Mersey and the Manchester Ship Canal at Bollin Point near Lymm.

Turn right along Waterside, along the side of the mill, then under the overpass to the steep road junction with Windmill Street. Turn left here and walk up the hill, stopping at the next road right, Calamine Street.

50. CHARLES ROE'S COPPER WORKS & WINDMILL / BETHEL BAPTIST CHURCH. Charles Roe opened his copper works here in the 1750s. A plan to link the works to the Mersey Docks at Liverpool via a canal through Kerridge and Poynton was defeated by the Duke of Bridgewater whose canal between Manchester and the Leeds & Liverpool Canal at Worsley had opened a short time before in 1758. Part of the copper works was converted for use as a Baptist Chapel in the late eighteenth century and bought by the congregation for £750 in 1822. The attached Sunday School was bought in 1857. Windmill Street was originally Lunts Hill Road but was renamed after Charles Roe's water pumping windmill that was sited near here. It was later adapted for grinding corn and eventually removed to Kerridge where it continued to be in use until the end of the nineteenth century. It was dismantled in the 1940s.

Continue along Windmill Street to, on the left:

51. **ST. PETER'S.** Despite its style, this church was built as recently as 1849. The style, like St Paul's (64), is Victorian Early English, although the dormer windows are unusual non-standard characteristics. A spire was originally intended for the offset southwest tower which itself was not completed until 1910. The exterior walls are of local Kerridge stone. The congregation formerly met in a wooden building behind the Beehive Inn on Black Road (across the football field).

St Peter's (51)

And, opposite:

52. WORKING MEN'S INSTITUTE. A grim looking building dated 1875.

Continue along Windmill Street. On the right is

53. MACCLESFIELD COMMON. This football field is all that remains of Macclesfield Common which once covered much of this part of the town.

Black Road Scheme No. 1 (54)

The first road on the right after the football field is the

54. BLACK ROAD IMPROVEMENT SCHEME No. 1. When local architect Rod Hackney could not obtain a £20 grant from the council to replace his wash-basin he decided to take action, saving the row from demolition and initiating a scheme by which the residents renovated their own homes providing labour and a quarter of the costs. Improvements were carried out between 1972 and 1974. The terrace was built between 1812 and 1815. Rod Hackney lived at no. 222.

Continue along Windmill Street to the canal bridge, and

55. THE MACCLESFIELD CANAL. One of the last British waterways to be built, the Macclesfield Canal was designed by Thomas Telford and opened in 1831 to link the 15 miles between the Peak Forest canal at Marple and the Trent & Mersey canal at Kidsgrove, thus giving a direct link from Manchester to the Potteries and completing the 'Cheshire Ring'. The canal was a considerable work of engineering and the only locks on the entire route are at Bosley, near Congleton. The entire navigation within the Macclesfield District (from Middlewood to Bosley) was designated a conservation area in June 1975.

OPTIONAL EXTRA:

56. TOWN VIEW. This is a worthwhile diversion if you have the time. Continue up Windmill Street and bear right along Hollins Road. This road bears sharp left past the golf club. Stop at the wall on the right about fifty yards from the golf club. Return to the canal bridge.

Join the canal and walk along the towpath with the canal on your left. Just beyond the next bridge, on your left, is the

57. SITE OF QUAY FOR COPPER WORKS. The only canal crane left in Macclesfield can be seen here on the far bank in the back yard of new houses. Coal was unloaded here for Charles Roe's Copper Works on Windmill Street (50).

Leave the canal at the next bridge, turning right onto Black Road. A little way along, you come to:

58. **BLACK ROAD IMPROVEMENT SCHEME No. 2.** Also instigated by Rod Hackney, this was the second of the two Black Road Improvement Schemes. The houses were renovated by their residents between 1975 and 1979.

Return to the canal and continue in the same direction. Almost immediately on the right is:

59. **THE TOLL HOUSE**. This belonged to the Macclesfield Canal Company to enable the collection of tolls for passing cargo boats. A swing bridge was installed beside the road bridge and the metal runner for this can still be seen by the towpath.

Further along, on the opposite bank is:

60. **THE HOVIS MILL.** The mill was built in 1820 and the famous Hovis germ flour was first made here in 1885. Milling moved to Trafford Park, Manchester, in 1914 but the building continued to be used as Hovis' print works and publicity office. Milling returned for a while during the Second World War after the bombing of the Trafford Park premises. It has been proposed to convert the buildings to apartments and/or an hotel.

Leave the canal at the next bridge joining:

61. **BUXTON ROAD**, which was completed and opened for traffic in 1836. There was a toll bar near the canal bridge. There were a large number of open cast coal mines in this area until the end of the nineteenth century.

The Hovis Mill (60)

Cross Buxton Road and turn left (uphill) to:

62. ROAN HOUSE WAY. Designed and built by Rod Hackney on once-derelict land, almost entirely from recycled materials, an excellent example of conscientious modern architecture.

Head back down Buxton Road, crossing the canal, and take the first road left, Union Road. This road becomes Brook Street. On the corner of Brook Street and Turnock Street (on the left) is

63. THE INDUSTRIAL SCHOOL, which was situated here. The "Ragged School" for vagrant, orphaned, fatherless or neglected children was started here in a disused wheelwright's shop in 1858 by some of the St Paul's congregation. About a hundred children were taught to read and write and given a daily meal. Those who were over eight years of age were given jobs such as knitting and clogging and religious instruction was given on Sundays. The premises were renovated and expanded, mostly due to donations including £500 from the Marquis of Westminster, and rebuilt in a Venetian-Gothic style in 1866. It is now converted to industrial use.

Continue along Brook Street and cross, before the traffic lights, to:

64. ST. PAUL'S, which is a commissioner's church, that is, one built with Government assistance. £1,000 of the total cost of £5,400 was donated by the commissioners. It was built with local Kerridge stone in 1843-4 to serve the rapidly expanding town. This is the only remaining church in ecclesiastical use in Macclesfield that retains its spire and is built in the Victorian Early English style favoured by commissioners (see also Hurdsfield Holy Trinity, Bollington St John's, Macclesfield St Peter's (51) and others).

Return to and continue along Brook Street. Cross the Silk Road and turn left at the T-junction with Sunderland Street. This leads back to Park Green. Continue straight across the junction at Park Green to Park Street. On the left here, on the corner of Lowe Street, is

65. MACCLESFIELD REGISTRY OFFICE, an early nineteenth century building which is very busy throughout the year.

Take the next left, Lord Street. To the left is

66. MADS LITTLE THEATRE. The Parsonage Street Chapel (42, visible across the end of Lord Street) procured a Sunday School here in 1822 that was used for silk twisting during the week. It was pulled down in 1869 and the existing building was built in its place. The building was bought by Macclesfield Amateur Dramatics

Society in 1965 and substantially refitted by the members in the early 1980s. It is the only venue for regular live theatre in the town and plays host to many local and touring companies besides MADS' minimum thirty performances a year.

Continue along Lord Street to the next right-hand corner (Chapel Street) and find

67. BRUNSWICK WESLEYAN METHODIST CHAPEL, which was built in 1823-4 and enlarged in 1850. Its future is uncertain.

Brunswick Sunday School (68)

Next door, along Chapel Street, is the

68. BRUNSWICK SUNDAY SCHOOL. Built in 1823 (concurrent with St George's across the road (69)) it has been converted into apartments.

Cross St George's Street. Diagonally opposite the Lord Byron (named after the poet who died in 1824) is:

69. **ST. GEORGE'S.** This church is still the parish church of Sutton, despite the swallowing up of the old village by the new town in the mid-eighteenth century and the construction of St James' in Sutton Lane Ends in 1840. One of only three churches built in Macclesfield with classical elements, St George's has an unusual north-south alignment. It was built as St George's Independent Chapel for Protestant Dissenters in 1824 but came under episcopal authority and was consecrated in 1834 when the chancel was added to reflect the change in the type of service held. A splinter group had left in 1827, worshipped for a while at Townley Street Chapel (32) and built Kidd's Chapel (now the Salvation Army Citadel (82)) in 1829.

Walk along St George's Street (with St George's church to your left). On the left here, look for

70. **WEAVERS' GARRETS.** A fine row of a common sight in Macclesfield - three storey weavers' cottages. The top storey was used as a workroom for weavers and sometimes stretched the full length of the row with an exterior staircase. A large window for light was important.

Continue along St George's Street. On the right after Grapes Street is

71. **ST. GEORGE'S STREET BAPTIST CHURCH.** A fine example of a nonconformist Victorian chapel, built in 1873-4 to replace the Baptist Church on Calamine Street (50) which is still in existence. The attached Sunday School was a later addition. The interior of this church was used by the BBC for scenes in the serial "Mr. Wroe's Virgins" in 1992.

St George's Street Baptist Church (71)

Continue following St George's Street, bearing left by the railings and crossing the top of High Street to

72. HARVEST PRINTERS. Opened as another nonconformist church, Park Street Chapel in 1836, it has been in use as a print works for many years.

Continue past the printers and take the first left along James Street, then the second right along Chapel Street. Turn left along Peel Street, and cross to

73. 69 PEEL STREET. A parish boundary stone can be seen here dated 1780 with **M** on one face for Macclesfield (Parish of St Michael) and **S** on the other for Sutton (Parish of St George). This area was once part of Ryle's Park, the 241acre farm of John Ryle, silk and cotton manufacturer, banker and Macclesfield's first Methodist Mayor. Other, later, boundary stones can be seen in this area.

Return along Peel Street to Park Lane. Turn right onto Park Lane and here, on the right, is

74. **PARK LANE TERRACE**. This fine Georgian terrace was built in 1832 and restored as part of the High Street area conservation scheme in 1987.

Opposite is:

75. **MACCLESFIELD EQUITABLE PROVIDENT SOCIETY**, established in 1855 when five weavers collected capital to set up a business, bought a barrow-load of goods at wholesale price and re-sold them to themselves. Their first permanent premises were in Sunderland Street and this building was constructed with typically Edwardian ornamentation in 1908.

Equitable Provident Society (75)

Go down Nelson Street (by the side of the Equitable Provident building), then left into Vincent Street. Where B & Q now stands was the site of

76. THE PREMIER CINEMA. Macclesfield once had six cinemas. The first was the Palace (later the Regal) opened in Duke Street in 1910, followed by the King's Hall Picture House, King Edward Street, in 1911; the Picturedrome, Chestergate, in 1911 (now a bingo hall); the Cinema, Buxton Road, in 1912; the Premier, Vincent Street, in 1919 and the Majestic, Mill Street, in 1922. Only the Majestic remains.

Continue along Vincent Street and first right into Brown Street. On the corner of Brown Street and Statham Street (second road on the right):

77. BROWN STREET MILL. This was built as a silk mill in the 1820s.

Continue along Brown Street to:

78. THE BREWER'S ARMS, which was first mentioned in 1825. It was owned at the end of the nineteenth century by Hordern's Brewery of Lord Street who sold it by public auction to the North Cheshire Brewery. It was later owned by Ansell's and Tetler-Walker, both parts of the huge Allied/Carlsberg-Tetley organisation. The Victorian brewer Peter Walker of Warrington is commemorated by the pub's unusual double-sided sign.

Brown Street becomes Bridge Street, continue along here until you reach, on the right:

79. PARADISE STREET. This splendid row of renovated and modernised garret houses was built in 1826-7, adjoining the similar styled houses on Bridge Street that had been built in 1825. The last garret weavers were still active in this area until the 1930s. These garrets were threatened with demolition in the mid-seventies but were saved and restored by Macclesfield Borough Council.

Return to Bridge Street and continue until the road begins to dip.

80. **THE BRIDGE** that gives the street its name was probably located here, passing over Dams Brook (see also 30). This area was known as "The Dams".

Continue to the next road right. On the corner here, is:

81. **BRIDGE STREET MILL.** The first mill on this site was built for silk throwing in 1810 and, by 1841, there were four silk manufacturing firms on the premises. The Davenport silk firm, established since 1848, took part of the premises in 1890 and were the sole occupants by 1910, occupying the whole site. The old mill was destroyed by fire caused by a lighting strike in 1938, the current mill was built as a replacement the same year.

Continue along Bridge Street. Take the next right along Roe Street. Along here on the left, is the

82. **SALVATION ARMY CITADEL.** Built in 1829 by a splinter group from St George's Independent Chapel for Protestant Dissenter's (69) (who had worshipped for a time at Brunswick Wesleyan Methodist Church (67)) and known as Kidd's Chapel after its founder and minister from its formation until 1880, this is one of only three churches in Macclesfield with classical elements. Services ceased in 1926 when it united with Frost's (Park Green) Chapel (45) to form Macclesfield Congregational Church. The building was then used as the parochial hall of St Alban's (91) before being taken over by the Salvation Army who had previously occupied the Theatre Royal on Catherine Street which was destroyed by fire in 1931. Exterior scenes for the BBC series "Mr. Wroe's Virgins" were filmed here in 1992.

Salvation Army Citadel (Kidd's Chapel) (82)

Return to the junction with Bridge Street. On the corner is

83. **BAND'S THE BUTCHERS**, virtually unchanged since it was opened in the 1930s.

Turn right along Bridge Street. Turn first left along Waterloo Street West. On the corner, you find:

84. **65 BRIDGE STREET, BIRCH HOUSE.** Built in the 1830s as two private houses, Birch House has had a varied life. At the time of the 1841 census, half of it was occupied by Thomas Broderick, a silk manufacturer who owned Bridge Street Mill (81) and was one of the original trustees of Christ Church (85). The other half was a girls' boarding school that functioned until 1893. It was later used as a Socialist Club, the headquarters of the local Labour Party, the headquarters of the National Federation of Building Trades Employees, an architect's practice, the centre for the Air Raid Patrol service during

World War II and the centre for the local vets during the foot and mouth epidemic of the 1960s.

Band's , The Butchers (83)

Opposite is

85. **CHRIST CHURCH.** The construction of only the second church of any size to be built in Macclesfield, Christ Church, built in 1774-5 and opened on Christmas Day 1775, was funded by Charles Roe to serve the expanding population of the town. Some of the cost of the construction was recovered by Roe by the selling of plots in the graveyard for graves and vaults. The church closed in 1985 and is being restored with assistance from the Department of the Environment, English Heritage and Macclesfield Borough Council for both parochial and ecclesiastical use.

Fairstead House, 36 Bridge Street (86)

Continue along Bridge Street to the crossroads. On the right-hand corner here is

86. 36 BRIDGE STREET, FAIRSTEAD HOUSE, is the oldest house on Bridge Street, dating from 1790.

Diagonally opposite, you see the

87. MODERN FREE GRAMMAR SCHOOL. A business-oriented offshoot of the more traditional King's School (94), opened in 1844. It amalgamated with the King's School in 1910 following a Board of Education inspector's report (of 1904) that criticised the school for being under-equipped. The building was later used variously as a lodging house for schoolmasters, a dentist's, a children's clinic and free dinner hall, a Registrar's office, and is now the town's Education and Careers Offices.

Continue along Bridge Street and right into Church Street West. Stop behind the petrol station. Just here is

88. OWL HOUSE. Despite heavy restoration, this building is still recognisably Methodist. It was built in 1842.

Return to Bridge Street, turn right and see, opposite:

89. THE DRILL HALL OF THE 8TH CHESHIRE RIFLE VOLUNTEERS, built in 1871 by public subscription of one penny per brick. The clock tower and entrance hall were added in 1872. This date and "8TH C.R.V. DRILL HALL" are inscribed on the door surround. The hall was used extensively as a meeting place and centre of entertainment from its inauguration, including orchestral concerts, variety shows and circus visits. It continued to be used by military volunteers. The 7th Battalion of the Cheshire Regiment (Territorial Army) was based here from its inception in 1908 until its disbandment in 1967. The Hall is now used for trade purposes.

The Drill Hall (89)

Continue along Bridge Street, take the first left into Chestergate, stop at the traffic lights. Here stood:

90. THE WESTERN TOWN GATE. The road to Chester starts here and the town gate once stood close to this junction (hence Chester Road and Chestergate).

Bear left at the traffic lights along Chester Road. Along here on the left is

91. ST. ALBAN'S. This was only the second Catholic church to be built in Macclesfield after Henry VIII's break with Rome (the first was on the same site from 1810 and an earlier mission room was situated in Backwallgate). St Alban's was built between 1839 and 1841, over three hundred years after the formation of the Church of England, and was designed by A.W.N. Pugin (1812 - 1852) who later won the competition to design the Houses of Parliament in London. The church is a good example of a Victorian attempt at the Perpendicular style of architecture (popular mid 14th - mid 16th centuries), but it is a pity that many attempts to complete the tower have failed.

Return along Chester Road, back to the traffic lights, and bear right along Chestergate. Just before the next traffic lights is, on the right,

92. CHARLES ROE HOUSE, reputedly the home of Charles Roe, this building dates from the 18th century and was saved from demolition in the mid-seventies and extensively renovated. The extension behind was added in the late 1980s.

Take Little Street, almost opposite, and across to King Edward Road, to, on the left:

93. ALMS HOUSES, dated 1927 and renovated 1992-3,

Charles Roe House (92)

Alms Houses (93)

And beyond:

94. THE KING'S SCHOOL. The Macclesfield Grammar school was one of the earliest foundations, originally opening behind St Michael's church in 1502 (11), and received an endowment and a charter dated 1552 constituting it "The Free Grammar School of King Edward the Sixth in Macclesfield". It was re-sited to King Edward Street in 1748 and to this site in 1856. Only the central Gothic portion dates from this time. It was amalgamated with the Modern School (87) in 1910, was expanded between the wars by the construction of a science block and library and became a public school in 1938.

King's School (94)

Cross to the King's School side of Cumberland Street heading right, cross the top end of Hibel Road (take care, this is a busy road) and pass into the truncated part of Cumberland Street. On the right along here you find:

95. MACCLESFIELD SPIRITUALIST FREE CHURCH, formerly a Methodist church, built in 1879.

Continue along Cumberland Street to the junction with Jordangate. On the corner is:

96. CUMBERLAND HOUSE. The eighteenth century house (built in 1723) of John Stafford, who was the Town Clerk between 1748 and 1754. The Duke of Cumberland, second son of George II, stayed here in December 1745 in pursuit of Bonnie Prince Charlie. The house was renamed in his honour and when Cumberland Street was built in 1866-7 the street took the name of the house.

97. **JORDANGATE** was named after the 14th century mayor of Macclesfield and keeper of the castle gate Jordan de Macclesfield. The northern town gate was here on the left.

Turn right, towards the Town Hall. On the left, you can see:

98. **JORDANGATE HOUSE.** Built in 1728 and once known as Pear Tree House, this grand early Georgian town house was, from the mid-eighteenth century, the home of the wealthy Brocklehurst family of mill owners. The first John Brocklehurst took over Acton & Street Ltd., a firm of button manufacturers, in 1745 and was a major shareholder in Charles Roe's copper works. His son, John (1755-1839), changed the firm from button-making to throwing silk and commenced the production of woven silk for which the firm became famous. His son, John (1788-1870), was the first MP for Macclesfield and held the post continuously from 1832 to 1868, refusing a baronetcy three times. The Brocklehurst mill in Macclesfield was the largest silk mill in the country. Brocklehursts were mayors of Macclesfield seven times during the nineteenth century.

Further along, on the left, stands

99. **MACCLESFIELD LIBRARY.** The elegant buildings of the Manchester, Liverpool & District Bank Co., dated 1881, were restored and extended as Macclesfield's new library in 1993 and opened in March 1994.

And, opposite:

100. **THE MACCLESFIELD ARMS.** A coaching inn where fourteen year old Princess (later Queen) Victoria and her mother the Duchess of Kent stayed in 1832 on their way to Chatsworth. The Royal Telegraph departed from here every evening at six o'clock passing through Leek, Ashbourne, Derby, Loughborough, Leicester, Market

Harborough and Northampton on its journey to the White Horse on Fetter Lane, London. It is planned to restore the building as offices.

The Library (99)

Turn right into King Edward Street. The three-storey building on the left with the classical portico on its left side is:

101. THE MACCLESFIELD BANK, established by three members of the Brocklehurst family in 1816 (see also Jordangate House (98)) this was Macclesfield's first successful banking concern. All banks, except the Bank of England, were privately owned well into the nineteenth century and the success of such establishments depended largely upon the stability of the owners' private fortunes. The Macclesfield Bank was amalgamated with the Manchester, Liverpool and District Bank, who had a branch in Park Green (34), in 1891.

Macclesfield Bank (101)

Go through the portico and down the passage to:

102. KING EDWARD STREET UNITARIAN CHAPEL, the oldest dissenting chapel in Macclesfield, dating from 1690, shortly after the passing of the Toleration Act that granted freedom of worship to nonconformists. It was commonly known as Brocklehurst's Chapel after its patrons (see also Jordangate House (98) and Bank (101)). Very similar chapels are in Knutsford and Dean Row (Wilmslow).

Return to King Edward Street, turning left from the passage. On the left, along here, is:

103. STUART HOUSE. Possibly the ugliest building in Macclesfield, this was once used, ironically, by the Council Planning Office.

Opposite is

104. 19 KING EDWARD STREET, built in 1798 for Francis Beswick, a silk manufacturer and then mayor. His initials (B.F.E) and date of birth (1758) are on the rainwater heads. The house was later occupied by Joseph Tunliffe, a silk manufacturer who endowed the infirmary to the town and is now Grade II listed. Restoration as offices is planned. The extension next door is dated 1927.

Take the alley opposite (next to Stuart House). On the right here, notice:

105. THE BATE HALL. Built in the late sixteenth century, the Bate Hall was home to the Parliamentarian Stopford family. Oliver Cromwell, Lord Protector from 1649 to 1658, is said to have stayed here. It has been an inn since the eighteenth century. The Chestergate side has been refaced, but the original interior remains.

The Bate Hall (105)

Turning right from the alley by the Bate Hall, walk to the junction of Chestergate and Churchill Way. On the right-hand corner, at the junction, is the

106. FLYING HORSE INN, now divided into two, this was once Macclesfield's most famous coaching inn and closed in 1919.

On the south side of Chestergate (opposite the Flying Horse Inn) is a

107. TIMBER FRAMED HOUSE, dating from the seventeenth century, now split into three shops.

Timber-framed house, Chestergate (107)

Return along

108. CHESTERGATE, which has always been a popular trading street. Most of the buildings are eighteenth century. Looking above the modern shop fronts will testify to this. Chestergate was pedestrianised in 1988.

At the end of Chestergate is the Town Hall (1).

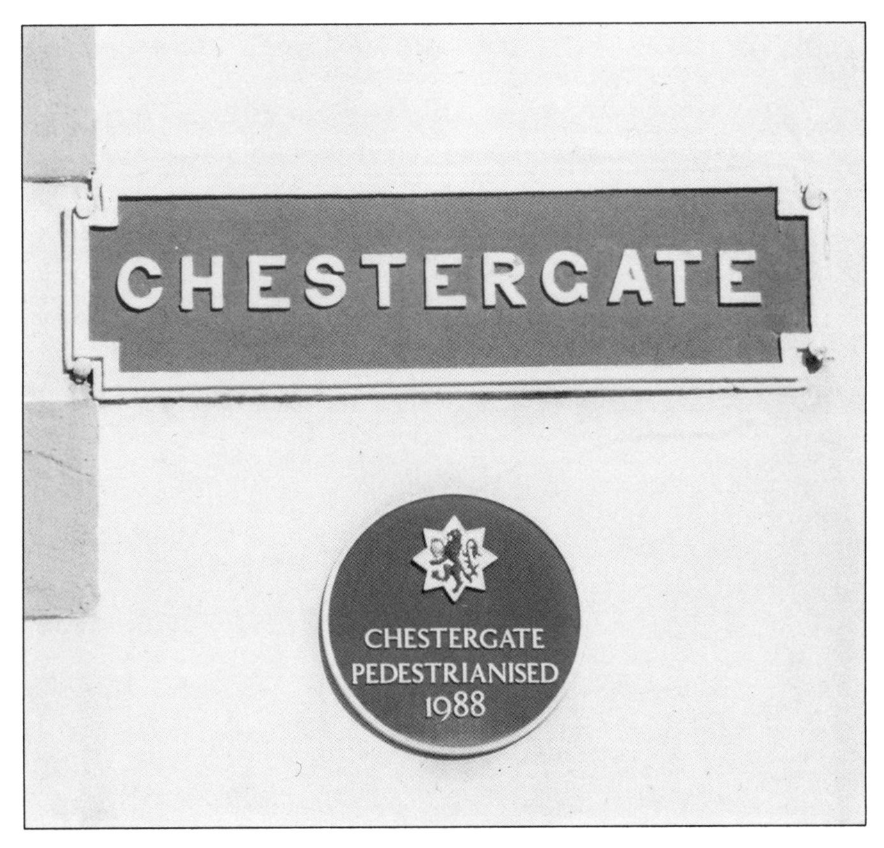

Chestergate (108)

Seven Shorter Walks

Although the main '108 Steps' walk can be completed in instalments, some may prefer to tackle these shorter walks. Please note that the numbers in brackets refer to locations on the main walk, and you will, therefore, need to refer to these numbered entries for further information. Likewise, parts of these circular walks make use of the main walk and, to avoid repetition, you are referred back to the appropriate linking sections.

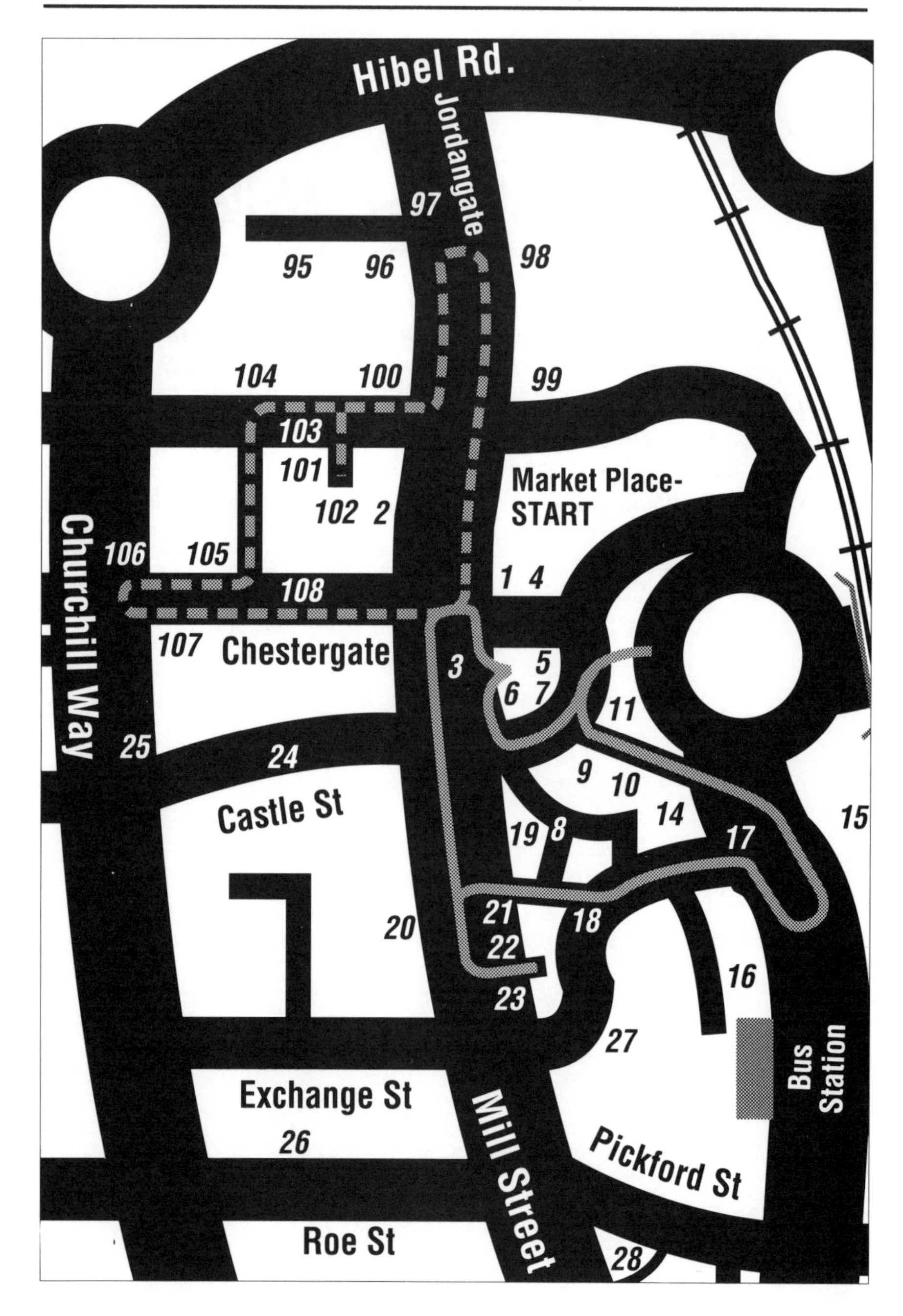

Hibel Rd.
Jordangate
97
95
96
98
104
100
99
103
101
Market Place-
START
102
2
Churchill Way
106
105
1
4
108
107
Chestergate
3
5
6
7
11
25
24
9
10
Castle St
14
15
19
8
17
21
18
20
22
16
23
27
Bus
Station
Exchange St
Mill Street
26
Pickford St
Roe St
28

1. Old Macclesfield: walk 1

This walk starts and finishes at the Town Hall (1) and is the solid line on the map on page 68.
Approximate duration: 25 minutes.

Follow the Main Walk from Town Hall (1) to Macclesfield Castle (23), then

Return to and turn right along Mill Street, which leads back to the Town Hall.

2. Old Macclesfield: walk 2

An alternative walk that also starts and finishes at the Town Hall (1) and is the dotted line on the map on page 68.
Approximate duration: 20 minutes.

Starting at the Town Hall Information Centre, with your back to the door, head along Jordangate to the right, walking as far as the junction with Cumberland Street. Cumberland House is on the corner here.

Follow the Main Walk from Cumberland House (96) to Chestergate (108) and back to the Town Hall (1).

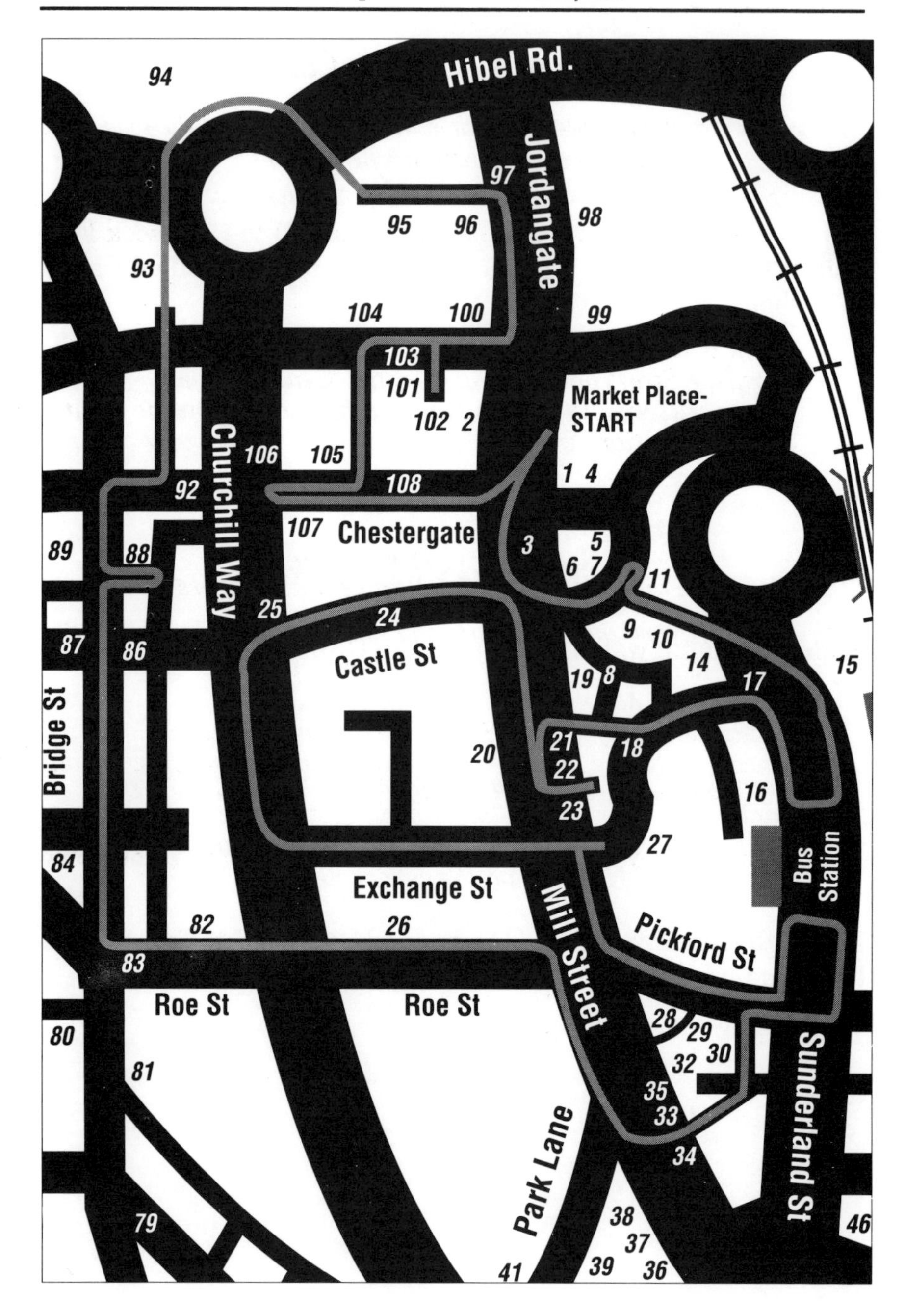
Hibel Rd.
Jordangate
Market Place-
START
Churchill Way
Chestergate
Castle St
Bridge St
Exchange St
Mill Street
Pickford St
Bus Station
Roe St
Roe St
Sunderland St
Park Lane
94
97
98
95
96
93
104
100
99
103
101
102
2
106
105
1
4
92
108
107
3
5
6
7
11
89
88
25
24
87
86
9
10
14
15
19
8
17
20
21
18
22
16
23
27
84
82
26
83
80
28
29
30
32
81
35
33
34
79
38
37
39
36
41
46

3. Macclesfield Town Centre

Again, start and finish at the Town Hall.
Approximate duration: 1 hr. 30 mins.

Follow the Main Walk from the Town Hall (1) to Chadwick Free Library (38).

> *Walk back along Mill Street (uphill), turning second right into Roe Street passing the Heritage Centre. Cross Churchill Way. Take care, this is a busy road. On the right is the Salvation Army.*

Read about the Salvation Army Citadel (82).

> *Continue along Roe Street to Band's the Butchers*

Follow the main walk from here to the Drill Hall (89).

> *Continue along Bridge Street, turn first right into Chestergate and continue to Charles Roe House which is on the right before the traffic lights.*

Follow the Main Walk from Charles Roe House (92) to the Town Hall (1).

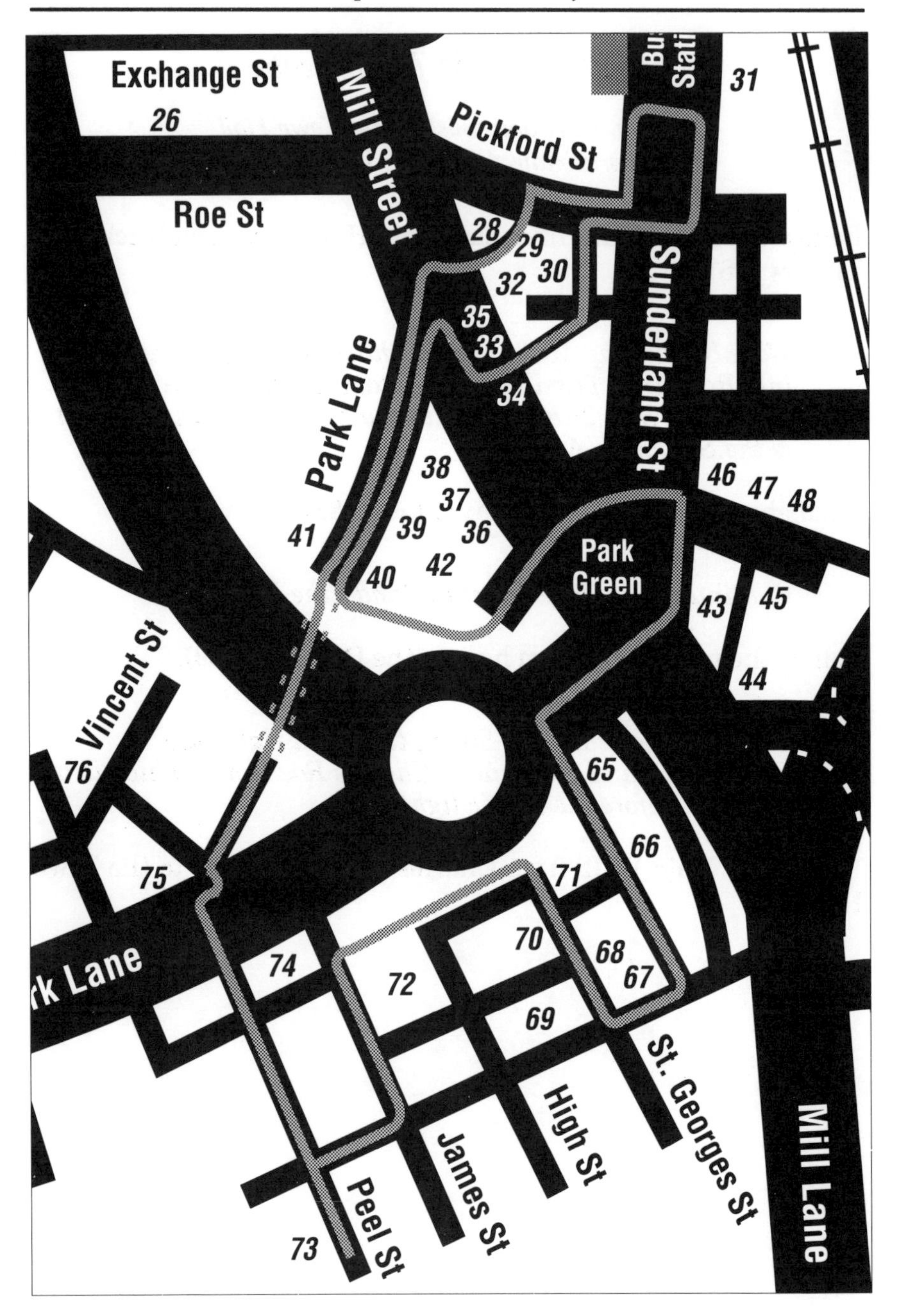

Exchange St
26
Mill Street
Pickford St
31
Roe St
28
29
30
32
35
33
34
Sunderland St
Park Lane
38
37
39
36
41
40
42
46
47
48
Park
Green
43
45
44
Vincent St
76
65
75
66
71
70
68
67
74
72
rk Lane
69
St. Georges St
High St
James St
Peel St
73
Mill Lane

4. Park Green

Start and finish at Macclesfield United Reform Church (33).
Approximate duration: 50 minutes.

Follow the Main Walk from Macclesfield United Reform Church (33) to the Silk Union Building (48), then

Cross the main junction to Park Street heading towards the grey and brown brick of London and Manchester House (the only road from the traffic lights which has an incline). On the left, on the corner of Lowe Street and Park Street is Macclesfield Registry Office.

Follow the Main Walk from here (65) through to Macclesfield Equitable Provident Society (75).

Cross Park Lane, keeping right, following the row of shops, then under the overpass and along Park Lane. Cross straight over into Wood Street (now pedestrians only) to its junction with Pickford Street. Wood Street Mill is on the right-hand corner here.

Follow the Main Walk from here (29) back to the United Reform Church (33).

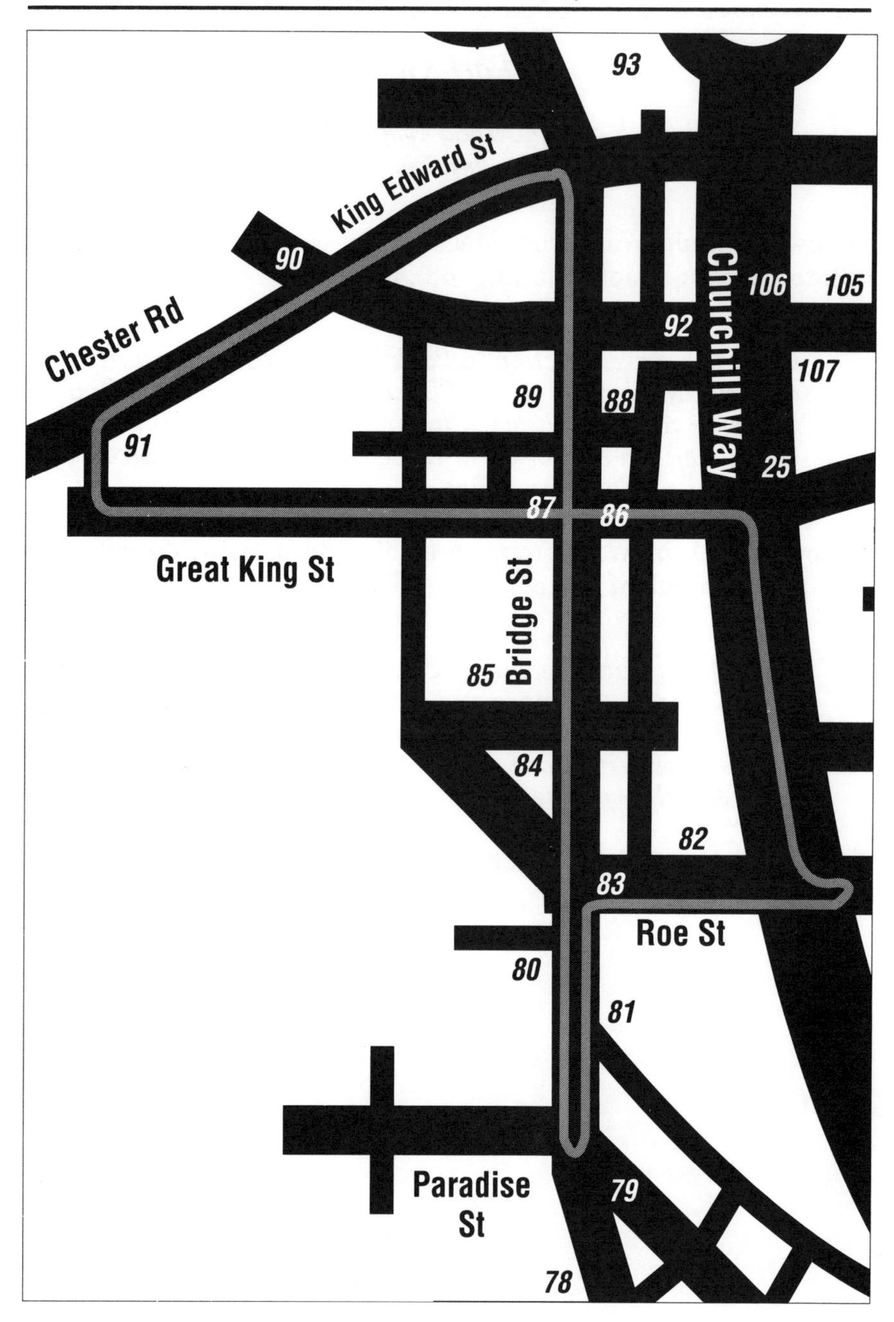
93
King Edward St
90
Chester Rd
Churchill Way
106
105
92
107
89
88
91
25
87
86
Great King St
Bridge St
85
84
82
83
Roe St
80
81
Paradise St
79
78

5. Christ Church

This starts and finishes at Roe Street Heritage Centre [Roe Street side] (26).
Approximate duration: 40 minutes.

Read about Roe Street Heritage Centre (26).

Cross Churchill Way (the main road next to the Heritage Centre), continuing along Roe Street to the Salvation Army (on the right).

Read about Salvation Army Citadel (82).

Continue along Roe Street to the junction with Bridge Street. Turn left and walk to Paradise Street on the left.

Read about Paradise Street (79).

Return to Bridge Street and turn right, as though you were returning the way you came, then,

Follow the Main Walk from Dams Bridge (80) to Bridge Street Mill (81).

Return to the junction with Roe Street, then

Follow the Main Walk from Band's The Butchers (83) to St Alban's (91).

Walk to the rear of the church and head back to the town centre along Great King Street, crossing straight over crossroads with both Catherine Street, and Bridge Street. Turn right onto Churchill Way and back to the Heritage Centre.

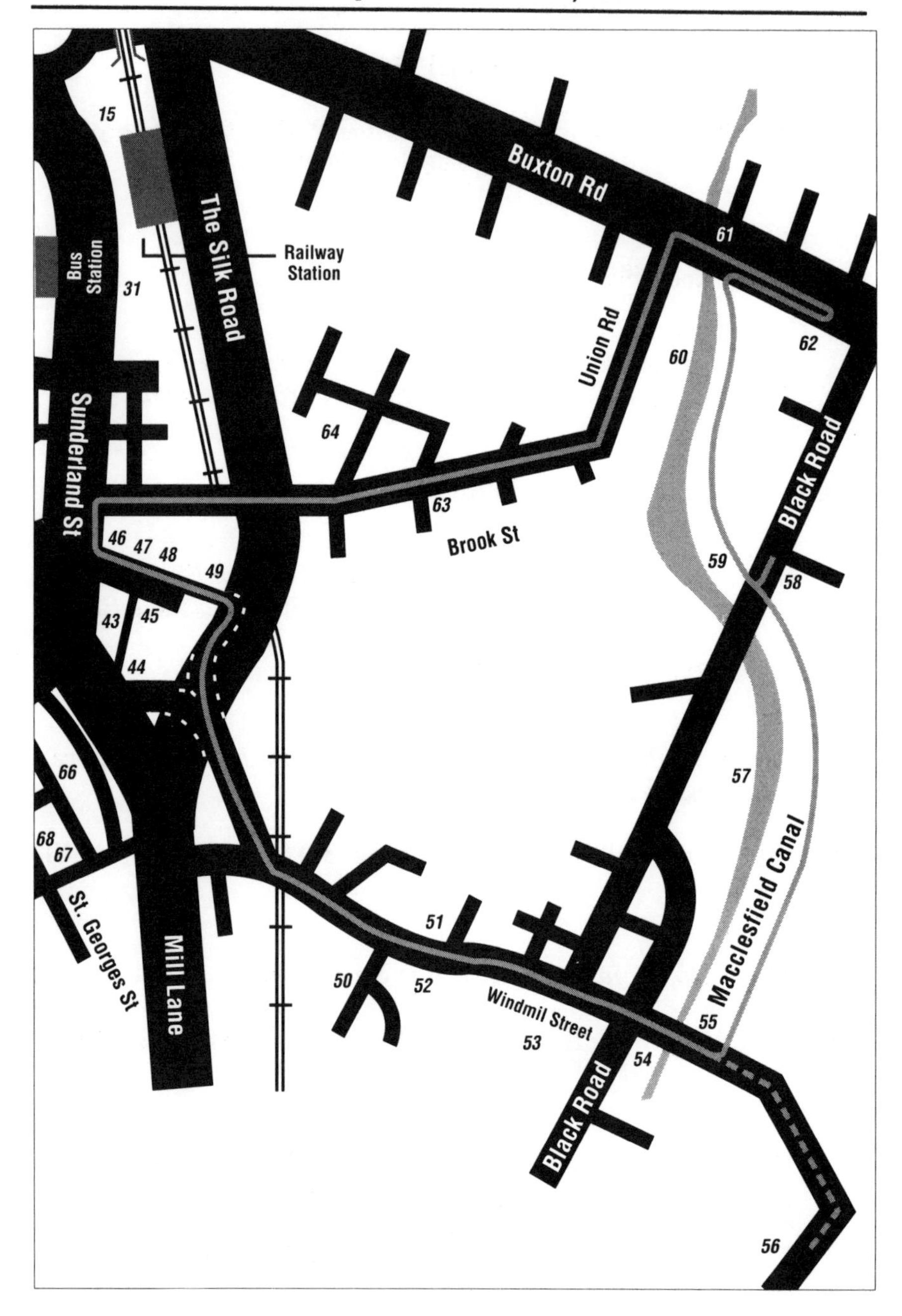

Buxton Rd
The Silk Road
Railway Station
Bus Station
Union Rd
Sunderland St
Brook St
Black Road
Macclesfield Canal
St. Georges St
Mill Lane
Windmil Street
Black Road
15
31
46 47 48
49
43
45
44
64
63
60
61
62
59
58
57
66
68
67
51
50
52
53
54
55
56

6. Black Road and Macclesfield Canal

The walk starts and finishes at Park Green War Memorial (43).
Approximate duration: 45 minutes.

Follow the Main Walk from Park Green War Memorial (43), back to Park Green (after 64).

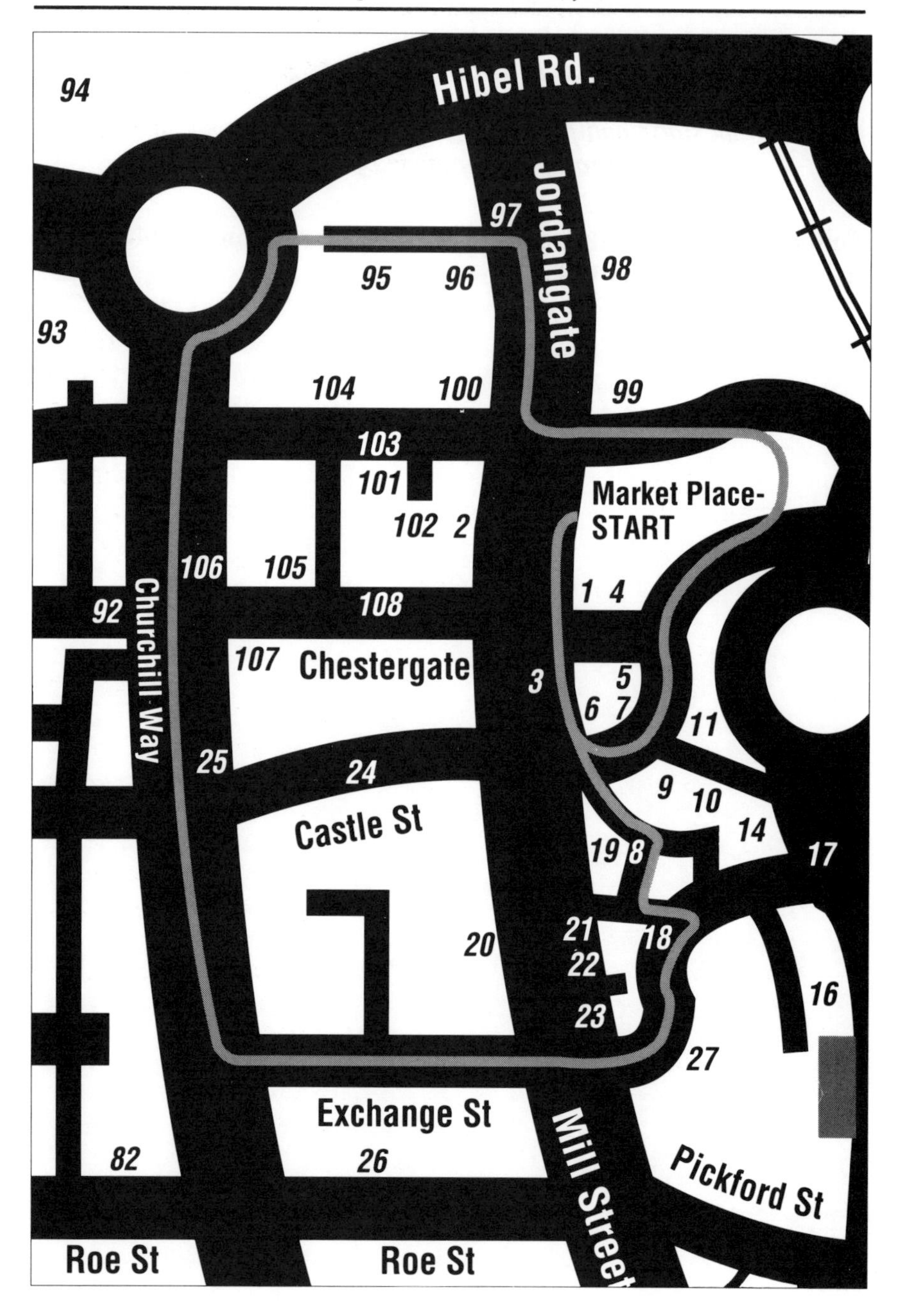
Hibel Rd.
Jordangate
Market Place-
START
Chestergate
Castle St
Churchill Way
Exchange St
Mill Street
Pickford St
Roe St
Roe St
94
93
97
95
96
98
104
100
99
103
101
102
2
106
105
1
4
92
108
107
3
5
6
7
11
25
24
9
10
14
17
19
8
21
18
22
20
16
23
27
82
26

7. Medieval Macclesfield

The start and finish is the Town Hall.
Approximate duration: 20 minutes.

The centre of modern Macclesfield is defined by the layout of the medieval town. The highest point of the town is the Market Place which stands on the apex of a rocky cliff that drops to the east. This drop was much steeper in the Middle Ages when the Bollin ran through a wooded gorge. Another steep slope dropped northward just beyond where Jordangate House now stands and, less steep, south to the Dams Brook which passes under Park Green. There was a ditch around the western part of the town. The following walk attempts to follow the fifteenth century town boundary.

Start at the Town Hall with your back to the door. Turn left and walk past the Town Hall and the church into cobbled Church Street which drops towards Waters Green. When Church Street turns sharp left continue straight on past the Castle and left down Backwallgate. At the bottom of Backwallgate turn right along Queen Victoria Street, then cross Mill Street into the partially pedestrianised Exchange Street. Turn second right onto Churchill Way, and follow this road, crossing Castle Street, Chestergate and King Edward Street. Turn right into the truncated Cumberland Street here, progressing to the T-junction with Jordangate. Turn right into Jordangate and then second left into Brunswick Street. At the top of Brunswick Hill turn right along the narrow alley between the three-storey house and the garage. Keep left along the side of the car park to the low wall and continue along here to the rear of the church. Circle the church with the building to your right as far as the church gates, then keep straight on back to the Town Hall.

Macclesfield Environmental Awards

The annual Environmental Awards scheme is organised by the Macclesfield Civic Society in collaboration with *Community News*. Requests for nominations are published in the *Community News* and awards may be presented to any building or other work of environmental importance completed during the previous year within the old (pre-1974) Borough of Macclesfield.

Choice of subject is wide. It may be a new building, a restoration or improvement of an existing feature or landscaping. If an interior is nominated it must be one to which the public have access. Apanel of judges consists of two Civil Society members, the Conservation Officer of Macclesfield Borough Council, the secretary of Macclesfield Chamber of Commerce and Industry and the editor of *Community News*. Presentation of the Awards is made by the Mayor of Macclesfield.

The figures in brackets reference the locations featured in *108 Steps Around Macclesfield*.

1982	Wellerby Court, Riseley Street
1982	Fyttons Shop, Chester Road
1982	Salvation Army Citadel (82)
1982	Harlequin Restaurant, Chestergate
1983	MBC Housing, Richmond Place
1983	Broken Bank, Lowe Street
1983	Arighi, Bianchi (12)

1983	Arighi, Bianchi (12)
1984	Cheshire Building Society, Castle Street (25)
1984	Trinity Home for the Elderly, Riseley Street
1985	Paradise Mill, silk weaving shed (40)
1985	Paradise Mill, Office (40)
1985	MADS Little Theatre, Lord Street (66)
1986	Heritage Centre (26)
1986	Nos 1-7 Chester Road
1987	High Street enclosure
1987	High Street / Mill Road housing
1988	Heritage Centre Assembly Room (26)
1988	Nevitts, Waters Green (17)
1988	Step Hill
1989	County Chambers, Chestergate (108)
1989	Chestergate pedestrianisation (108)
1990	The Old Millstone Inn, Waters Green (17)
1990	108 Steps (14) & Sparrow Park (11)
1990	Michael Dale's Studio, Mill Lane
1992	19 Church Street
1992	73 Great King Street
1993	Alms Houses, Cumberland Street (93)
1993	Macclesfield Castle Stones (23)
1993	Park Mill, Hobson Street
1994	4 Water Street
1994	St George's Playground, High Street
1994	Macclesfield Library (99)

Index of Locations

MUNICIPAL BUILDINGS

PUBS & INNS

TOWN FEATURES

3.	MARKET PLACE
14.	108 STEPS
17.	WATERS GREEN
23.	MACCLESFIELD CASTLE
43.	PARK GREEN

CHURCHES AND CHAPELS

5.	ST. MICHAEL'S
6.	SAVAGE CHAPEL
7.	LEGH CHAPEL
31.	WESLEY'S CHAPEL
28.	FRIENDS' MEETING HOUSE
31.	WESLEY'S CHAPEL
33.	UNITED REFORM CHURCH
42.	PARSONAGE STREET CHAPEL
45.	FROST'S (PARK GREEN) CHAPEL
50.	BETHEL BAPTIST CHURCH
51.	ST. PETER'S
64.	ST. PAUL'S
67.	BRUNSWICK WESLEYAN METHODIST CHAPEL
69.	ST. GEORGE'S
71.	ST. GEORGE'S STREET BAPTIST CHURCH
72.	PARK STREET CHAPEL
82.	KIDD'S CHAPEL
85.	CHRIST CHURCH
88.	METHODIST CHURCH
91.	ST. ALBAN'S
95.	SPIRITUALIST FREE CHURCH
102.	UNITARIAN CHAPEL

STREETS

8.	CHURCH STREET
10.	ST. MICHAEL TERRACE
18.	BACKWALLGATE
20.	MILL STREET
24.	CASTLE STREET
61.	BUXTON ROAD
79.	PARADISE STREET
90.	CHESTER ROAD
97.	JORDANGATE
108.	CHESTERGATE

HOUSES

9.	43 CHURCHSIDE
13.	VICTORIA PARK FLATS
46.	PARK GREEN HOUSE
47.	GEORGIAN HOUSE
48.	SILK UNION BUILDING
54.	BLACK ROAD No. 1
58.	BLACK ROAD No. 2
62.	ROAN HOUSE WAY
70.	WEAVER'S GARRATTS, ST. GEORGE'S STREET
73.	69 PEEL STREET
74.	PARK LANE GEORGIAN TERRACE
84.	65 BRIDGE STREET, BIRCH HOUSE
86.	39 BRIDGE STREET, FAIRSTEAD HOUSE
92.	CHARLES ROE HOUSE
93.	ALMS HOUSES
96.	CUMBERLAND HOUSE
98.	JORDANGATE HOUSE
103.	STUART HOUSE
104.	19 KING EDWARD STREET
107.	TIMBER FRAMED HOUSE

SCHOOLS & SUNDAY SCHOOLS

SHOPS

MUSEUMS

MILLS

WATERWAYS & RELATED BUILDINGS

30. THE DAMS BROOK
49. THE BOLLIN
55. MACCLESFIELD CANAL
57. QUAY FOR COPPER WORKS
59. CANAL TOLL HOUSE
80. DAMS BROOK BRIDGE

THEATRES & CINEMAS

66. MADS' LITTLE THEATRE
76. PREMIER CINEMA

BANKS

34. BARCLAY'S BANK
99. DISTRICT BANK
101. MACCLESFIELD BANK

OTHERS

15. RAILWAY STATION
27. EL RIO DANCE HALL
52. WORKING MEN'S INSTITUTE
53. MACCLESFIELD COMMON
56. TOWN VIEW
75. EQUITABLE PROVIDENT SOCIETY
89. DRILL HALL

The Redundant Churches Fund

Parish churches are a familiar and beautiful part of the English scene that they seem to be as permanent as the landscape itself. Sadly this is not so. For a number of reasons, such as the mobility of the population of the town and the decline in church attendance, many of them cannot now be maintained for their original purpose: the Church of England no longer has a need for them and they are redundant as regular places of worship.

Some redundant churches are found other uses - as places of worship for other denominations, as concert halls, cultural centres, offices or houses - and some are demolished; but there are others which are so important to the nation that their preservation must be secured. It was to look after churches of this kind that the Redundant Churches Fund was established. Almost three hundred churches have been preserved in this way, including Christ Church, Macclesfield.

The Fund's main income is provided by the Department of National Heritage and the Church Commissioners. Donations can be made to the Redundant Churches Fund, 89 Fleet Street, London EC4Y 1DH (Registered Charity No. 258612).

The Redundant Churches Fund

SIGMA
Leisure